TENDER

Selected Poems

Laiwan

Talonbooks

Talonbooks
9259 Shaughnessy Street, Vancouver, British Columbia, Canada V6P 6R4
talonbooks.com

Talonbooks is located on xʷməθkʷəy̓əm, Sḵwx̱wú7mesh, and səl̓ilwətaʔɬ Lands.

First printing: 2020

Typeset in Arno
Printed and bound in Canada on 100% post-consumer recycled paper

Interior design by andrea bennett, cover design by Typesmith
Cover images: compilation of works from Laiwan's ongoing project "she who had scanned the flower of the world …" (1987 to present)

Talonbooks acknowledges the financial support of the Canada Council for the Arts, the Government of Canada through the Canada Book Fund, and the Province of British Columbia through the British Columbia Arts Council and the Book Publishing Tax Credit.

Canada | Canada Council for the Arts | Conseil des arts du Canada | British Columbia | British Columbia Arts Council — An agency of the Province of British Columbia

LIBRARY AND ARCHIVES CANADA CATALOGUING IN PUBLICATION

Title: Tender : selected poems / by Laiwan.
Names: Laiwan, author.
Identifiers: Canadiana 2019019099X | ISBN 9781772012514 (SOFTCOVER)
Classification: LCC PS8623.A3975 T46 2020 | DDC C811/.6—dc23

bark odes or bark owed
how to recompose clean lines
in body burden times?

—Rita Wong, *Forage* (2007)

FOREWORD

by Debora O

Within the contours of Laiwan's book lie field notes from a life lived across multiple affinities, kinships, and desires. Both textual and visual, it is a beautifully complex collection of experiences and reflections spanning thirty years of curious inquiry into our shared human–animal condition.

TENDER is a book that traverses diverse terrains – the body, land, language. It is rooted in the courageous and uncompromising history of activism and in experiences of building community across and beyond difference. Within its pages is a radical and decolonizing cleansing of all that oppresses and alienates.

In the words and images of this collection are revealed the heroic struggles of gendered, raced, and sexual difference from a place of incredible tenderness and vulnerability. Laiwan's words imprint in us the need to breathe our animal skins back to life after the scarring of dehumanized, fearful states of abandonment and betrayal.

Read as a retrospective and as a continued call for a passionate caring for one another, *TENDER* offers us freedom in the face of limitation: a *working at setting free.* Each section of this collection captures a moment in time and feeling. Haunting, political, and defiantly sexy, Laiwan's voice is a guiding force. Ghostly images are choreographed to leave us alerted to longing and hope, absence and presence. It is as if the entire collection were a garden at different stages of growth, with the inevitable decay and renewal that each season brings.

In her imaginings we as readers retreat and renew our courage to speak – and breathe – anew.

on heroics

1997

feeling

For many years I have been preoccupied with throwing out The Heroic. That which is of persons from someone else's value: Cecil John Rhodes, the Pope, Vasco da Gama, Mother Teresa, Christopher Columbus, Jesus Christ! How do I find someone to call my own?

Most heroes who were fed to me since kindergarten are difficult muses. I snarl their names with reluctance as a reference point. What was their heroic act: our idea of them having done something of *extreme courage*? Their names are here to remind me of their *exemplary action,* told to me in a way to inspire a sentimentality, my inadequacy ... our redemption.

I do not *feel* like remembering. Such stories, the actions of these *heroes,* have taken up so much time and space they inspire a grand nausea in me. A hollow feeling at the base of the gut. As if to say: Remember feeling? Forget remembering ... feel this.

voice of the body

Strong, silent, princely kiss: *i swallowed a poisoned apple for this?*

If *feeling* is a language, how and what have I been taught to articulate?

The amount of time I have taken to clear myself of The Heroic is equal to the space The Heroic has taken in my body in dis-ease and symptom: an equation I've learnt to unmute my hesitant body.

heroic action

Attending to *feeling* as it is happening is extreme courage. It is where the likes of nausea can exist, grow, and be communicated. To communicate this dis-ease. A dis-ease that comes from knowing there is a *motive,* a mission, as to why someone is teaching you about The Heroic.

Taught to be awed by The Heroic *and yet bored by alienation* – I embodied a double bind of conflicted passion: *a silencing of feeling. In the closet.*

Extreme courage is an attention to dis-ease without compromise.

heroic icon

Before I knew that there is a difference between men and women. Before I knew as a girl that my desire would be considered a particularity particular to women: I saw *him* fit into a place of desire in my imagination. A lithe, graceful body of movement without excess. Feline, suave, and intent.

Lee: he had the same surname as my aunts. Bruce Lee: known throughout the African continent as the iconographic chinaman. A chinaman with the perfect guerrilla skills for surviving in the colonies. Skills ancient and perfected by the infamous Wong Fei-hung who fought invading foreigners in China at the turn of this century. Wong Fei-hung: heroic solely among the Chinese signifying the *selective heroics* of wars, politics, imagination ...

At twelve, smuggled into a rhodesian drive-in, I saw for the first time Bruce Lee's precise leaps and philosophy of body existing in a place of perfect timing, perfect choreography, perfect self-defence. Sidestepping assault to reuse the misspent *ch'i* of the boring and untrusting. An articulation of body that could be mine.

Like the only iconic *cinematic chinaman* I knew of, I too wanted to be a street fighter: a boy with position. I wanted to be the butch philosopher: a fighting drag king. One who knew that the punch came from a place of passion – not anger nor sorrow – "from the heart, with *feeling*," he had said.

Desires my aunts warned me about.

defiance

In contemplating the *heroic act,* I think of how often *boredom* and the ensuing compromises strike. Aeroplane food, junk mail, telephone surveys, the job of packing chickens every day, top-ten radio. Hierarchy, jealousy, mediocrity, repetition, predetermined being, unkept promises, predictability: *boredom.* Social control through dullness. How do we defend ourselves?

Perhaps a most *heroic act* is that which defies, with intent to defeat, *boredom.* A decision which refuses to accept the averaging of being to the lowest expectation or creativity. Such defiance, such a choice is an intense *desire* based on the belief in *value: i am worth more than this!* Without selfishness but with *a longing for freedom* – a belief in liberation.

back to body

If creativity is rooted in the desire to free all that has been silenced and/or institutionalized: it is where we face the fear of *feeling* – a signifier of *woman*, all body unheard and predetermined for all genders.

Where I was raised, apartheid rhodesia, I am made invisible for womanness, chineseness, for *not* passing in drag: a body that cannot exist. It is where my feeling is mute, all response to the external masked. *A smuggled body.* When I visit this place, imagination and creativity cannot exist outside of me – it is expression without venue, dulling *desire*: a hiding of passions, instilling the nausea that is a cabin fever of the closet …

Unmuting their undoing, taking care of this body that was not allowed / is not loud: *working at setting free.*

feeling again

Sometimes when I'm bored, I think of the work of a body's T cells. Fighting disease and infection, they multiply or subtract in calm or in battle.

And I think this multiplication or subtraction against infection is *a heroic act*: a passionate blood. *Working at setting free.*

notes towards a body I

(mozambique)

1998

i once believed
compassion could only originate from memory:

what did i forget?
why did i forget?
who had i forgotten?
why are you forgotten?

mozambique

memory in the body
ocean a body, remembering every crashing wave

there is the absurd
a ship crashed beside a lighthouse
ideology of navigation and science on the rocks
every crashing wave
marking this site: a memory of misdirected exploration

these images are not about beauty

this is a place that has never existed
never permitted to exist
some one else's desires invade

mozambique:
a generation of body being burnt
a generation of nose and ears cut off
marking this site:
a memory of misdirected exploration
some one else's war with your body

skeletons along the shore
        how did we forget?

we learnt to navigate unknown territories
        with awareness and spirit stopped

        body shrivels as memory shrivels

a body of money without memory
a body of memory without money
        who shall i be?
        skeletons in my closet

mozambique
        hot days where time stopped
        night of fierce wind and ocean swallowing
lighthouse, shipwreck, a generation of roaming children

i spent days absorbed by this sand that changed every moment
like my understanding changed every moment
like the war tactics changed every moment

the ship keeps revisiting and repeating the crash

i once thought only memory can revive my compassion
i once thought only compassion can revive my body
i once thought only body can revive my memory

mozambique
what am i forgetting?
a generation of people wanting body back

to whose advantage is forgetting?

a mythology from the earth

1986

water steaming from the sun : early-morning sun
steam as flames being thrown : flames of water
"you are earth in womb," she said

not yet with steam nor flame, we speak through
blood and bile and spine
"you are my room," i said

with the love of earth, i hold and push, tug and gasp
her hand is rough : she causes me to hold my breath

surviving and warm as leaves of the mulberry tree rustle
green, surrounded by hedge and cloud and sky

her hands washed my face in motions that kept
my eyes clean and my heart direct

we walked this path to the pomegranate tree
she showed me the seed. she showed me the sprout

she shows me the love of earth : the root of perception

and from the sky
i imagine her bathing in steam : flames of water

and from the sea
i imagine her diving for anemone and dulse
and water laps against her
moulding her clay into a shape of smooth
strength and rock

her heart taught me my heart was a muscle :
a muscle made stronger by hers

her muscle taught me battle and persistence
struggle in the face of lacking air and
foreign strangleholds

and from the air
she showed me the land on which to walk firmly
the direct line of the magnetic compass

the magnet of meaning

north south east west shrouded by fog

she teaches me the yell of a foghorn
she teaches me the howl of surrender
she teaches me the silence of our presence

learning to listen, i hear her breathing
she whispers command. she words poetry. she speaks
words i do not know and other words so direct and frank
i absorb strength and
frighten myself

learning to smell, she feeds me scent by scent.
lily, peony, lemon grass, chrysanthemum, poppy, wild rose.

i smell the soil in her sweat
she gives me a scent that is mine : fuel for fire

Night

learning the caress of eyes
i look at her and i forget myself

i see only immense stars and bright planets amid darknesses
the birth and death of light : the source of heat and warmth

i look at her and i am overwhelmed by heat and light

she looks at me and she irons out the creases
she looks at me and i become : as if being breathed upon

she expels the sight of despair .

i saw the flames of her skin in the dark
nightshade room and i held my hands out to them

i saw the flames and was scorched by insatiable curiosity

i held out my hands again, palm open
she breathed on them to harden and flex their labour
and from this, they inherited a story of their own

in the palm of her hands, she gave me fire
and taught me to forge

the forge of initiative and independence
shaped by heat and water and resistance

shaped by touch and tenderness

i imagine her in her garden at night
preparing seedlings under an endless sky

i imagine her at ease and concentrated

from these trees
i hear her collecting sounds in a box

and she plays these to me during sleep :
blowing a wind to lighten my flesh

i am flying in my sleep
without time, without space
just clear blue water below me

it is she who has taught me this

each day she gives me a word

from these she shows me the world
where land and ocean and love exist
where my heaven and purgatory are created
and sadness becomes a shadow

from these words she teaches me the grammar of play
spellings from anatomical and cellular desire
we're giggling like small children
discovering the syntax of sensuality

my hand held her dress as we waded through
the shallows of the sea looking for starfish and phytoplankton
that day she made me float on my belly

and i learnt of fear
to see fear in all its capacities :
learning the capability to step-by-step and sidestep around them
so as to peer inside

"you will peer as habit," she said
and left me there to float

and in the night sky she brought out her
telescope and peered up to read the news

i touched her again and she resonated in the touch
i caught her fire on my skin and clothes
and her eyes smiling branded her image in me –
the chemistry of silver particles
the attraction of magnetic opposites

she moulded my character into a crude form
and with her hands in water

she smoothed the cells with electric fusion

i realized the world of crudity within my crude form –
of cities without sense, of consciousness in suspension

propelled now out of a world of calm and comfort :
of her lily, peony, lemon grass, chrysanthemum,
i learn a passion for the unknown and wondering –
shaped by her desire to see me draw myself,
through curiosity and muscle, this map of my own

her eyes branded her image in me

"the fire on the skin is the forge," she said :
the matrix of ignition

postscript: yangtze river (长江), china, 1986

down the gorge along these immense mountains of china,
the river runs faster as the width narrows.

along cultivated ridges of farming,
houses on the steep mountainsides scattered and
flying birds in quiet, expansive country.
fertile river to live beside. amazing steepness and
still the ability to harvest and plow mountainsides.

sound of the strong river water washing against the boat,
rocking with the rattle of loose metal pieces.
a powerful wind. the engine drowning amid the roar of water.
i am looking at the many specks of houses high above
with black shadow windows that make them appear abandoned.
the sight of the amazingly patterned farming,
ridges and ridges, sensual and luscious,
i suddenly understand i am witnessing an intensity of life.

sound of the water grows stronger
the wind stronger – a bond is tied.
it is with the land.

up ahead, grey blue mist of mountains set up between the brown
yangtze water and the pale blue sky. mist. birds. green surround.

a return.

solitary speckles high above me in coloured cloth. people. living.
simply. surrounded in the mountain. trees, and becoming trees. rock
near water. mud and rock and broken rock at silt. a few ruins. empty
shells of houses discarded. goats in mountains. water ox plow. i cannot
imagine the hardship of tilling this land. no machine can climb such
steepness. only human muscle.

breast mountain: the woman yangtze

woman triangular lap: the river came /

rain droplets. breeze. smell of soil and mud.
men carry coal up the side of the black hill in wicker baskets on their backs.
below them small coal boats. our boat swerves to and fro –
a thrill travels my spine. this smell of rain. freshness of air in green richness.
a man sings on the deck below – a song so familiar, and still i don't know it.
the water currents rage on. pushing us.

land overpowering the senses.
elements overpowering the senses.

i am greedy for you.

untitled I

2000

try to give a reason for having left
there is no reason in leaving

there could have been a choice
count how many times you're given a choice

one leaves when home is made a foreign place
this is never for you to choose /

moved by this body
propelled into an unknown

precarious with threat, betrayal, abandon
there is no good reason to choose precariousness

you may wish to never leave again
yet you may never have opportunity for such a thought /

there is no going back even if you did /

my ocean a body
remembering every crashing wave /

LUNG:
towards embodying

2008

Ambitious and weary of his barbarian princess Medea, Jason arranges to marry the daughter of the King of Corinth. The desertion and ingratitude of the man she loves rouse the savage in Medea and her rage is outspoken. Fearing her vengeance, the King banishes Medea and her two children to exile ...

I begin with a spin because each and every tale spun matches the machine we use, literally spinning 8×, 16×, 32×, 48× ... I join this spin, turning it into dance. I will spin words, weaving them to be a dance of words, turning meaninglessness towards an unknown, an unpredictability and lack of predetermination, so a meaning unveils itself without my individual will or intentionality.

A spinning dance with a spin of the body: a re-embracing of bodily being to counter our Cartesian trap of bodily obsolescence, sedentariness, and erasure of the values and inherent skills of somatic being. As the machine dances, it spins faster in every new version. So too are we spinning, bodiless, captured by the hysterics and neuroses of every crash and freeze caused by its lacks. With a laser Cycloptian eye, it scans for data while surveillantly adapting my every move to an informaniacal tarantella, with a heartless and futile pace.

I long for lung. Clear lung. Clarity. Not the moist, thick fog of a pneumonic constriction guided by the plaintive warning of a one-eyed Cycloptian lighthouse /

Instead I dream of the expansive lungs of open savanna, fields of dry, harsh grass cutting the skin with touch. Blossoms dried to prickly pear and brown brush rush bush. Of spiders clambering with a meticulous pace through their web to catch a pest of meaning, to eat, to nourish, to poison the gift of sentimentality, of do-wellers on a not-so-secret mission to do *good* – lecturing authoritatively to manage a citizenry.

"A hurricane is a hurricane and we've seen its devastation," said the Florida governor last night. It went in one ear and out the other and I thought nothing of it. At his podium, well dressed, every one-eyed Cyclops aimed to record his every word: it was made to appear as if he cared about "devastation," as if he bodily *knew* devastation. Then my lung-brain rewound and replayed and I registered how nothing was registering ... uh-oh, the numb lung of a televidual one-eye. What he said was too obvious to have meaning. Yet in media, this attention in itself, zooming into his image, represents profundity; he is to be profound, meaningful, even if mundane, inane.

Media, with its current pace and pant, are a fast spin of words and tales. Spinning a tale, chasing a tail – the propellation of the unthinking brawn of the one-eyed laser /

again, with a patrialogic to keep the citizenry in place /

To be un-numb is not to be a machine in a blind propellation. We see this increasing. Informaniacal collecting of data to direct our lives, our desires, our consumption, our future terrorists, our panic level. Ailing lung: a panic of fear (*allergy*), grief (*asthma*), and suffering (*pneumonia*). With a speed of ever-mutating bacteria and the sluggishness of a diseased bodily fatigue – a habituated consumption (I suggest *tubercolossal*) growing cells of fears, tears, grieving of what is lost, a panic about what is yet to come.

This is stressed lung / without breath / oppressed, unempowered / celluloidally *stress manifest* in the flesh / cutting immunity through helplessness, melancholia, Prozactal and Ritalinoidal glum / we resort to consuming self and others, of objects, informatics, instantaneous pharmacologics, retail therapy and other escapes / we unlearn the ability of tenacity: the tenacity of bodily duration and patience / the patience of a breath within a listening to an expansive temporality /

Yet, how do we imagine what is yet to come? How do we learn this imagination? Do we only know imagining by what as children we learnt or can we grow a new method, approach, syntax, vocabulary? An un-numb lung will not breathe numb questions or succumb to suffering or grieving silence. Instead, it is present, feeling, visceral, somatic, humorous (for laughter is belly-full), generous, empathetic, compassionate. Improvisational without plan or expectation in every moment. To not be machinative or pre-emptive – we had learnt this from the King who "pre-empted" any movement of Medea solely because of *his* fear; as from Jason, we learnt how to be ambitious *through betrayal* /

here then we return to quality of spirit, for it is the heart of our concern /

Chinese philosophy, as in *The Mustard Seed Garden Manual of Painting*, adapted here to apply to our subject, suggests: *the secret rests basically in the circulation of spirit* (ch'i yün) / *flowers should have a variety of positions: front, back, and side views* /to clarify, *if they are to make an agreeable composition, they should be placed naturally* (tzŭ jan) / *the hand should move like lightning; it should never be slow or hesitant* / to clarify, *the circulation of spirit* is whole-bodily not solely of vision, hand–eye, or cleverness and intellect / an understanding of "spirit" is that it is physical energy which includes one's vitality of character and is not from a religion of any kind: this must remain clear /

Vitalized character and un-numb questions are an agency of empowerment and a communal vision of the world for self and others. They question the pharmacological machine and its instantaneity in naming and administering chemical machines towards a numbing pathology: the panic of stress / diverting us from what is real, which is: breath / nothing else will keep you alive /

Every event and media is a phenomenon. I breathe each phenomenon into un-numb lung (*breathe in dark: breathe out bright*), investigate it, find its relationships and representations (*why this, now – what does it tell me of me?*), and with this, relate the appropriateness of the media to the context and content. Each machine is anthropomorphic in character, corresponding with and revealing values / consciousness, each of our values / consciousness: each choice we make mirrors us, character flaws and all – personal, societal, global.

Medea is of the world, alive, orgasmic, savage, straightforward, honest, and passionate with conviction. She is not in awe of telelogics and its distancing machinations. She will discard them at whim. Neither is she in a one-eyed spell. She spins a dance of her own. She redescribes clear fields of lush bush and fiery red twilight – enraged, engaged, critical, nurturing and nourishing a new curiosity: killing passivity, inviting engagement, collaborating in the world without the need to fix, own, contain, control, convert, or detain, but aspiring to a community of freethinkers who love monstrously and viciously to keep awake / while she, in turn, is loved /

A return of a new Medea, enchanting an alchemy of magical seduction, total bodily joy (an exchange of cells) *and / or wounding* (a revolutionary punctum with a graceful ch'i)*, to thrill, orgasmically a jouissance /*

ode to a ferocious thistle*

2009

* The scientific Latin name *Onopordum acanthium* is ultimately derived from the ancient Greek words *onos*, "donkey," *pordē*, "a fart," and *akanthos*, "acanthus," altogether meaning a thorny plant eaten by donkeys and causing a fart." The common name *cotton thistle* derives from the cotton-like hairs on the leaves; the name *Scotch thistle* comes from a legend that the plant's thorny thickets helped protect Scotland from the Vikings.

somewhere between
an underpass and an overpass
arresting me with her ferocity of independence

caught by the seduction of her solitude
she whispers gruffly "how am I here alone"

stopped in my tracks
breathing in this wonder
this gift of shocking beauty

complicated by uncountable threatening thorns
much too many more than needed
yet obviously earnestly necessary

she fends off touch
defending a tough sinewy taut stem
a stem spiralling single and visceral
tall confident and straight

lean and mean
proud of her complications
proud of her defences

proud of baring a shock of tender wisps
to crown all the subtly complicated prickliness

a crown so soft and light
such tender gentleness that needs to be fought for and protected
at all costs

her other crown with a slight downward gaze
pensive, a little sad, thoughtful

not to be picked, not to be poked,
not to be meddled with in any way

for any such attempt would explode her into flight
releasing her into the air
ruining the delicate balance
between fierce defence and ferocious vulnerability /

untitled II

2002

we know this well, ah paw / images and memories ours and also not /

when you arrived i was three / days sewing in the Hong Kong factory replaced with selling tea and bread to locals / on this voyage you brought almond and old wife cakes / tastes now my reminders of you and the old country

noisy streets with gates trying to keep us together / lived at once with pride and pain, in wealth of imagination and poverty of materials / shared with adaptability, improvisation, and ancestral spirit /

i remember the courtyard of our store cemented with memories of immigrant struggle / small chicks grew up here as laundry hung out to dry / to one side was a storage room where the workers lived, sleeping on cardboard for beds / cramped in apartheid without home /

on the other side was a tree that ba had brought from Mozambique years before / something i imagine to be like a Chinese magnolia with small yellow-white flowers / this sweetly scented magnolia, grappling also with colonial Africa, was caught between pavement, a brick wall, and the courtyard roof of corrugated iron that threatened to cut off its leaves / it stood alone in this little rectangle of dirt imagined by ba as a garden from China

beside this tree was another small courtyard where clothes were washed and we bathed / where mum grew her bean sprouts and the stray cats fought territorially for comfort

i remember before the bathroom was built how we washed, all us kids, one at a time, in the big metal basin / we were dusty and the pavement made us dustier /

here, i notice a solitude, a quietness, a history of my father and grandmother /

a depth of silence, something like survival /

we know this well / making do with what is left or what is allotted: improvise and adapt, play where you can /

this defiance, this insistence to be practical and bear quietly / pursued as an epistemology of our ancestors /

who has shown us to reconstruct this village in the back street? on this road less travelled, a corner we claim in a humble happiness of basic necessity / proud at the ability to make do with little /

arms crossed holding the chest together / bands across your cardigan also to keep it together, to keep heart from spilling / hands hidden to keep from telling too much, from having to deny having done anything

these three muses: Past, Present, Future / we know them well. the looking-back-just-in-case, the anxiety-of-where-we-may-fail or -for-what's-about-to-come / and then he, defiant and straightforward. eyes ablaze /

we will find you being threatened to change and move / relinquished as tastefulness erases your epistemology

yet every backstreet fertile the world over and every paved courtyard savoured for its reverie of possibilities

will find a magnolia growing today even in a rectangle of dirt /

notes towards a body II

1999

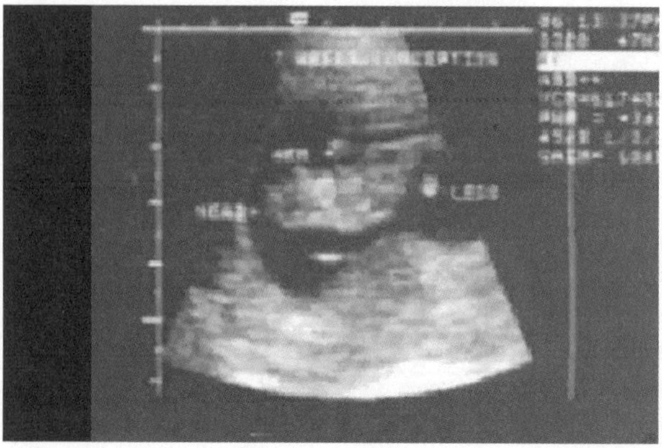

i am remembering the time i was not yet born
when there was no such thing as time
and no such thing as remembering

no, i am wrong
i remember, but not through memory

here in an image of being not yet in this world
a floating, bouncing, jumping shape, closer to cyborg than human

a pixelated mass where i am a life of something else
of dancing lights without body

in a cramped, unfamiliar, freezing space
which could be purgatory, limbo, nowhere
everywhere

this couldn't be me
this being couldn't

i can no longer feel her. i ignore her as she always available yields
mother, forgotten by a surge of inhumanity:
the one person who could know unconditional love so well
who could be my body of compassion
yields to forgottenness

i, waiting to be born, become remembered
solely by a frozen image of a frozen time
of the not-yet-born
of the still-being-born
of the still-being- and the stillborn

of a still life in portrait
longing for body

i am remembering mother's hands
no, this is not hers she is not here
not a part of this

could this be my hand? could this be of my hand?

do we regret contributing to this most dullening of deeds
of removing life from being itself?

holding onto mother
before i was born fists clenched
fearing nothing but the invention of time and being named
named by image, then frozen in space

compassion and memory and body
are shocked into silence
eliminated in the process

this couldn't be me
this being that couldn't

i remember, not through memory
i remember mother feeding me

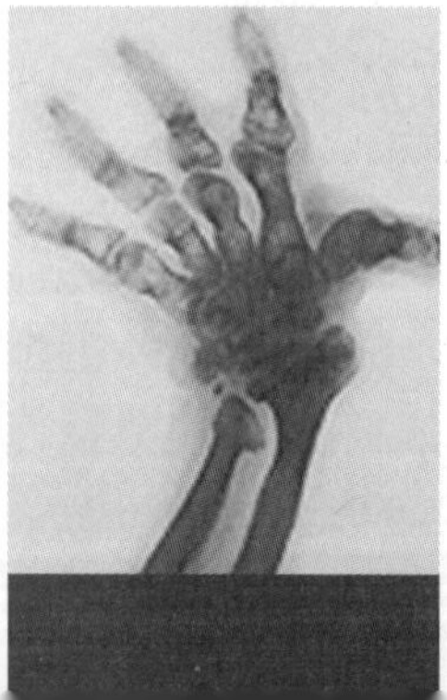

my memory a body
remembering every crashing wave

how can i come to know unconditional love

when desire comes in waves, a push-and-pull effect
drowning in an unknown, instigated by some karmic trick

i am going in, looking in
to see what i am made of

i once believed love originated from my mother's body
i once believed my body came from my mother's love

i once believed compassion could only come from remembering
this   my mother was my body

from where is the cause of my upheaval
this knotted gut
this gutted heart
this disheartened surgery of feeling?

outside of this condition, i am remembering unconditional love
in a body tremble or body sweat, i remember
gut feeling

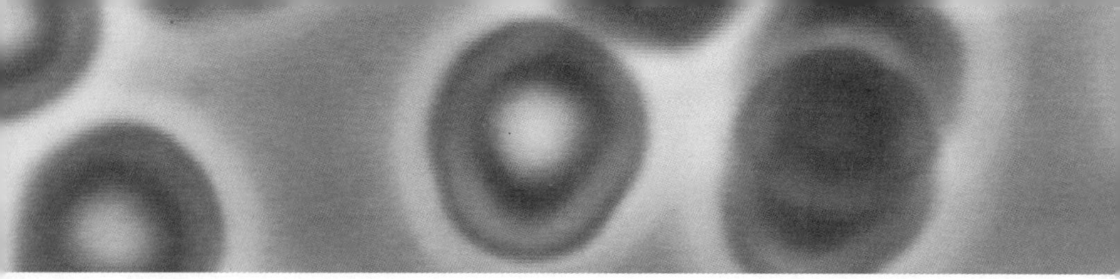

this is my body, this is my blood
no, i am wrong, this is a portrait of me

in all these processes
i have been searching for ways to bring some body back
mother, me, or past and future lovers

i am remembering the stillness of this moment
which reminds me of when i once had to be reminded of mortality, of body, of blood
of when i was reminded to be still

i look at her and remembering comes flooding back to body
blood rushes to circulate some kind of lightness
and day-to-day motion becomes derailed for this most invisible of flurries

still, i am breathing deeply
so as to never neglect
what her body is telling me   what my body is telling me
without words, without gesture
not silent, but telling in a rush of catching up

never forget
how telling this is: this rashness of blood circulating some kind of insistence
circumnavigating unconditionally a desire to listen to this that so reveals

this image: this is my blood
outside of me because i had forgotten

how telling she is

to gut and a rise

2002

September fourth two thousand and two

to gut

>>Canada's coast a "gateway for terrorists" / *how do they sleep at night?*
>> Clark's conflict report to become public / *these men who rule our world*
>> Petition demands coast guard changes / *soul trampled in blind ambition*
>> Leaky condos: one big lawsuit? /
>> Blast possibly a murder-suicide / *to calculate*
>> B.C. cutbacks force federal jail changes / *to control*
>> First day of school beset by problems / *to impoverish*
>> "Kids aren't performing": schools studied / *to abandon*
>> "Keep B.C. Hydro as it is," court urged /
>> Bus fare boxes tight squeeze for scooters / *he will try to police you, dear soul*
>> Logging OK'd on spotted owl habitat / *he will try to pierce you, dear heart*
>> Coquihalla pileup shows need for beds /
>> Our fire crews may be stretched too thin / *how does he sleep at night?*
>> "My heart is beating like crazy," says winner
of PNE prize home / *counting sheep he covets?*
>> Sexually abused foster children launch
class action suit against B.C. gov't / *dreaming*
>> Campbell urges caution on Kyoto / *of the next book to balance?*
>> The selling of 2010 begins in B.C. / *counting wives he desires?*
>> Oil-rig worker killed by black bear / *counting cars he'll own?*
>> B.C. prison to house female prisoners / *counting trees he'll clear-cut?*
>> Wife's death in Mexico "accidental" / *counting the days till his death?*
>> Woman, 63, hurt in crash with stolen car /

>> Anglican leader opposes split diocese / *there are*
>> UBC draws more foreign students / *three ways to "gut"*
>> Search for missing hiker halted / *one: to gouge out the*
innards of Being
>> "B.C. schools not relevant to most," Clark says / *so as to devour the other*
>> Kids head back to bigger classes today / *two: to gouge the heart of*
one's own Being
>> Private schools see little growth / *so as to suddenly feel*
>> Just nine days of rain this summer / *three: to be struck with*
sudden nausea
>> Long weekend claims 3 / *when realizing the consequences*
of one's actions

sadly, he doesn't know the last two

September fifth two thousand and two

a rise

>> Accused murderer tormented, in pain / *what will we be left with?*
>> B.C.'s "frugal" government spends a lot / *greed eats him and spits him out*
>> Teacher wins compensation for illness
caused by classroom stress / *emptied of meaning*
>> Dead parents moved to B.C. "for their kids" / *spiralling words*
>> Ottawa commits to city convention centre / *into endless rhetoric*
>> You're asked to take stairs on Sept. 11 /
>> Woodward's parkade to be redeveloped / *he is a dinosaur of pathetic proportions*
>> City shuts suspicious sidewalk
tax business / *a numb corporation of cells*

>> Tough-talking ex-cop seeks mayor's job / *a slave to money-grubbing ass*
>> Bombing suspect wants debt repaid /
>> Small SkyTrain blunder costs $200,000 / *he fucks himself furiously*
>> "She's a girl who has a dream" / *so as to take himself seriously*
>> HIV infection on the increase in B.C. / *eliminating compassion*
or ethics
>> Crown appeals ruling on assault charge / *coming violently only when the*
numbers crunch
>> Kelowna captives forced into prostitution / *when the books balance*
>> Labour says no to privatized Coquihalla / *when the homeless are*
more homeless
>> Report said Skeena in bad shape / *and he remains controlled*
>> Mother dies in hwy. car accident / *and he remains controlled*
>> Neufeld says Kyoto promise is nuts /
>> Class action suit filed against B.C. Hydro / *how is it he is so easily cruel?*
>> WCB jobs, services cut because of loss / *so easily without conscience?*
>> Canada's coast a "gateway for terrorists" / *so easily without*
>> Clark's conflict report to become public / *sense of consequence?*
>> Petition demands coast guard changes /
>> Leaky condos: one big lawsuit? / *it is no wonder*
>> B.C. cutbacks force federal jail changes / *youth and elders arise*
>> Times colonist behind picket line / *to end our rotting –*
>> First day of school beset by problems / *returning*
>>Logging OK'd on spotted owl habitat / *to this earth generous*
and listening

for honest emotion is the root
to all things.

what is a park

1996

like me, the boundary where *nature* becomes cultured or culture becomes *natured* is a blur. a process so quick to become forgotten.

a park is a memory. a memory of a space or place, of what our urbanized selves have no time for.

it is an unlearnt space, a space we knew in childhood, where ducks and frogs and trees and daisies and puddles were intimate with us.

unlearnt because we are no longer intimate with this space but approach it with practicality and control.

we may go to the park we feel intimate with. we may walk randomly and with spontaneity. we may walk without seeing the park at all. the weight in our heart may have brought our eyes in.

we may keep a park in our memory to remind us to be sane. there too, we can relearn to be intimate with little friends we meet.

a park is maligned if used solely as a refuge.

she is a reminder to wander without objective.

for intimacy is new every time.

whale

(contrary to shaping a permanence)

2002

my ocean a body
remembering every crashing wave

how it is i am moved
towards the inconsequential
knowing every swell and surge
needs no conditionality

yet, i have seen every moment
in a child's day scheduled

and grief has no boundary
until we see

beauty unafraid
to love in chaos
with curiosity and rigour

ungrasping
in constant search and motion

she is tall beside me
unbending in devotion
wordless with consistency

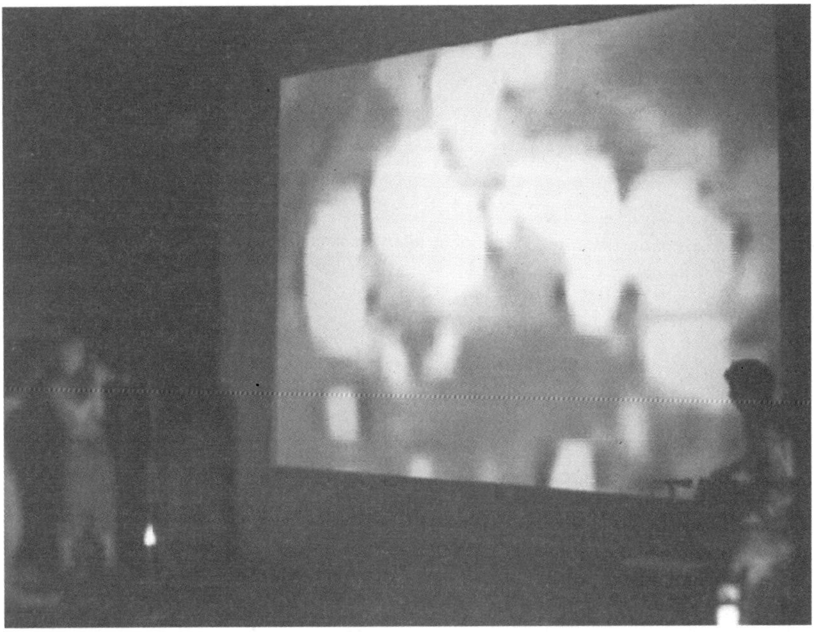

expanding breath
open to discover
what cannot be named
and can remain unsaid

in wonder /

untitled III

(poem for the week
after the summer solstice)

2009

we have relatives much smaller than eyes can see
so small we forget they are here beside us, faithful,
believing in our being

we relate as if we have forgotten them, forgetting
every day how they bring us to life, feed us, comfort
us

we forget how green and beautiful they glow in the
dark how they send us into smile and laughter /

we have relatives who live in every cell that make
our bodies where breathing has built our lives
around them

haunting our lungs with a freshness that shocks,
when we wake one morning in the middle of nowhere,
really happy

without care because we suddenly remembered
freshness and all our little relatives who have
clamoured together, to sing into each cell "hello?!
are you home?! wake up, ding dong!"

and you wished this would happen every day, not
only when your heart had suddenly gone into shock
feeling the deep ache

not only when larger relatives have gone to really
ignoring you, relatives so large we should not have
forgotten them, but we did

and now not caring, they're throwing a party that's
going to go on all night and all day, all night and all
day and all night and all day, with a lot of free-
flowing fluids, seas and oceans, that's going to
make it so you can't fall asleep for a long time

and those are only the grown-up relatives throwing
a party

wait till the kids break loose /

we have relatives who are so hungry as we kept all
the food in the larder locked up, saved for a rainy
day, but the rains haven't come because the grown-
up relatives, feeling ignored, decided to throw their
own party and the rains were invited there /

we may have run out of water for any more tears
we may have spilt all our blood for any more water
we may have run dry of excuses

we may not be able to be thirsty anymore because
our hearts have gone on strike, we're feeling hung
over from a bad binge that's gone on too long and
the rot has festered into the shell we built around
hearts and lungs

rusting iron heart shell
rusting iron lung shell

where we wheeze a wrench out of the works once
in a while out of lost impulse, lost spontaneity, lost
desire

but thankfully for rust eating away so loyally to free
heart, to free lung, yelling in "hey, you home?! wake
up, ding dong!"

rust, the loyal dog, gnawing away at that festering
bone, happy in the end to bury it, a job well done,
another armoured shell out of commission /

and there is heart, and there is lung, lying side by
side, patients in the acute care ward, suddenly
feeling everything, exposed and laid bare,
vulnerable

suddenly finding tears, thankful to find tears, fluid
and flow have returned

thirsty for breath, thirsty for love, parched with
chapped lips that would now kiss too deeply so
other hearts and other lungs would stand shocked
for how your liquids rip into their armour to rust
faster

all this desire and all this fluid, no wonder it was
locked up and kept for a rainy day, it drives us into a
frenzy of delight, of joy to be freed, with thunder
and lightning booming "happy freedom day!"

even if we have to stick it out a bit in the acute care
ward, getting bored out of our minds

that is the whole point, our minds had gotten their
way for this long

and now they must get bored, bored with
themselves

and in this suddenly see how heart and lung are
much more entertaining and delightful than we had
once thought /

thieves 1, 2, 3, 4

and

tender 5

2019

thieves

1.

time speeds past our hands
that have forgotten how to hold

soft from wringing anxiety
with a touch of the screen
with a handheld
with each time we're told to dial it down

with a softness of heart (like a muscle)
or softening of conviction
or soft timbre of voice (like a whisper)
or a soft tender of mind

like tender timidity
a fear to step out
with straight spine and tall walk

let it fall away

stop this plunder, pilfer, spin
and leave this portal behind

time sped again
we look to our hands and see what we had held

a toss of cavalier words, they call it a salad without bite

words promised
worlds promised

what have we done – anything? everything?

what is disappearing
what is appearing

there’s nothing more you can do to let a world be seen
like you holding still /

thieves

2.

we had convinced the world
to return the earth as flat

and we had convinced ourselves to live with everything flat

this convincing
was nice and polite and good with a virtue compatibly flat

comfortably flat

with a toe to the line to preserve what is flat
we had honoured further flattening and be flat further with fervour

flat out flat broke in nothing flat and we have fallen future flat

then they cut a tree around the corner to pave a way to get somewhere else
for one. single. man.

then hundreds of years in one split moment
a tree lay here in logs of even metre /

once rivers and mountains and curves
once children in soil among beetles and worms
the horizon was a line shifting and changing

where lungs breathed with gasps and laughs and sputtered emotions

we return, to tune in with long-lived skill, to each subtle turn of air
to be with ease in uncertainty /

thieves

3.

he punctuated each sentence to end with "sad"
a full stop, to a forced stop

a curse that breaks the path forward

no grieving
no mourning
but instead a decisive, emptying "sad"

thievery thrives each time "sad" sucks the wind out of us
just like the time he looks at you and says "smile"

thieves thrive when we can be robbed of imagining what could be imagined

they start this robbery when you are young
taking you from your mother
putting you in a stranger's house
leaving you to fend for yourself

then fending becomes the foundation for the rest of your life

the rest of us shrug with stupidity, dabbling in minor chords
diverted to an attempt at music that spits in dribs and drabs
one hundred and forty characters or less
splintered between "sad" or "smile" or pure rage

why this type of "sad," and why that type of "smile"
this mocking bullying "sad," that intimidating judgmental "smile"

diverted (i'm swamped by the anxiety to "smile")

forgetting who to stand with
betraying how we would mourn

he, predetermining this deadened "sad," that unhappy "smile"
punches out each breath we could be breathing

from words that once had feeling
become a fast curse against what was once civilization /

thieves

4.

that day he took me aside saying he wanted to know my story
midway he said, oh, that's just your version

without a word I walked away
stepping through another portal into a parallel world /

settlers with histories of sweltering dreams
powered by gaslight

discrediting the story you own, the ritual of your ancestors, teachings
now diagnosed as mistaken remembering

delusional, infants to be withheld, taken, reschooled, et cetera, ad nauseam

freedom
has been quietly slipped in between shelves
where toothpicks, plastic bags, toilet rolls, and jiffy scrubbers
with sixty-two-dollar cabbages and boil water advisories
exhaust freedom to a ghost's life

gaslight

jumbled into mixed-up categories
deliberately misfiled by identity, to misplace children
switched at birth or detained in cages
so that mothers will no longer be recognized

all this to make finding any future home elusive

to the horizon
we face an enraged sun and an outraged moon
blasting heat and fire, continent changing, flood and rise
to afford no more sentiment, no more romance

for the stars are unforgiving in this thieving light

where in ten years, one degree of added warmth
threatens a thirst where water will no longer form dew
where your tongue will no longer know how to call love's name
where tenderness would be scorched

where he promised us paradise
and he burnt everything /

tender

5.

our lifetime spent looking for home
thieves have come in, rearranged who you are
putting you out onto a stranger's doorstep

making you foreign to yourself

but there in the heat of a barren desert
a woodpecker made the door where a pygmy owl nests inside a prickly cactus
her little ones, small mirrors of herself,
tender in this enclosure

a cool aloe moist room of her own
lit by an incessant sun outside
lit into a pale blue-green
lit as a secret heaven

outside bristling thorniness appears not homely at all
a steadfast fierce to fend off

she does not ask for much
we do not have to do much – simply honour this, where she lives
stay away, do not pry, let her be

for this is the work of the decolonial
step back, make space

let others live
let others thrive

we must not need to have everything

and yet, and then

everywhere, in the most modest of moments
there is everything we could ever need

everywhere, in any given moment, millions of miracles occur

a cactus becomes a home

we learn to arrive home in every unique time and any unique place

we return to timelessness
we return to spaciousness
we return to emptying with a regular relearning

we return to the liveliness of breath, in every breath

to face what is right here
to face all we use, all we waste
to witness this in grieving all its horror,
the horror that is ours we've made and ours alone to own

so now, we count how little we need
a return to tender

once you are born, you enter a universe of a home
sextillions of stars, trillions of unknown galaxies

a woodpecker, a pygmy owl, a cactus, a desert, an ocean, a flower, a fruit, a furry coat

each welcome you

to move in this world with surprise in any given moment
into a pithy love that is tender and curious and with these companions /

she who had scanned the flower of the world*

1987

* The 1987 artwork *she who had scanned the flower of the world* is made up of fresh and dried vegetation, placed in glass slide mounts. It was originally installed in a gallery and, on another occasion, performed/projected for an audience. The title comes from a line by Sappho: "she who had scanned the flower of the world's manhood" ("To an army wife, in Sardis," in *Sappho: A New Translation*, trans. Mary Barnard [Berkeley: University of California Press, 1958, 2012]).

a celebration of spring, the coming of light and longer days. a metaphor
for a working psychic ecology. towards a sensual economy and
its embodiment

in winter
we learn to name the oppressor and the name becomes oppressive
this is the logic of repression

she who had scanned the flower of the world
finds an evolution according to the secret life of a typical dwarf yellow
star, the sun

in the spring twilight a full moon is shining
cell by cell i am devoured by light and heat
metamorphosis from one body to another
i become you

woman
muscle upon muscle, strength in strength
we will return with limbs of iron
with dark and furious eye
independent from words
shocked at the limits to growth

yet

you
a calm of soul
fragrance intoxicating
invading
taking me to a stillness without boundary

still to imagining
my garden with you

she, the speed of light in empty space

at this precise moment the cloud and sky open to emit light
at this very moment flowers open to exhibit an end to the unending
within one burning explosion
        moulded into emotion   every sensual realm exposed
molecule by molecule i am devoured by light and heat

without genuine affection where would i be?

IMAGE CREDITS

Unless otherwise noted, all photographs were previously published along with the poem in which they appear (see Acknowledgments on page 130) and are used with permission.

"notes towards a body I"
Pages 13–15: photographs by Tonderai Katiyo, ca. 1990.
P. 16: by the author.

"untitled I"
P. 36: by the author, adapted from a family photograph. Mozambique coast, early 1960s.

"ode to a ferocious thistle"
P. 50: by the author, 2009. Previously unpublished.

"untitled II"
Pp. 54 and 57: Sharyn Yuen, *340 East Cordova* I and II, 1983.

"notes towards a body II"
Pp. 60–63: public-domain photographs from anonymous photographers.
P. 64: micrograph of the author's red blood cells, 1999.

"to gut and a rise"
Pp. 66 and 69: by the author. House being demolished in East Vancouver, 2002; along Coquihalla Highway, south of Kamloops (Tk'emlúps), British Columbia, 2002.

"whale (contrary to shaping a permanence)"
Pp. 76–79: by the author, 2002. Live-performance stills from a video by John Fukushima.

TEXT CREDITS

The verbal and noun definitions of the word "tender," including the derivative "tenderer" and the phrase "plea of tender," that open this book are taken from *The New Shorter Oxford English Dictionary on Historical Principles*, vol. 2, *N–Z*, edited by Lesley Brown (Oxford, UK: Clarendon Press, 1993), p. 3247, and are reproduced with permission from the Licensor, Oxford University Press / Clarendon Press, through PLSclear.

Italicized passages in "LUNG: towards embodying" are quoted or adapted from "Book of the Orchid: Ch'ing Tsai T'ang Discussion of the Fundamentals of Orchid Painting," in *The Mustard Seed Garden Manual of Painting / Chieh Tzŭ Yüan Hua Chuan, 1679–1701: A Facsimile of the 1887–1888 Shanghai Edition*, translated and edited by Mai-mai Sze, Bollingen Series (Princeton, NJ: Princeton University Press, 2015), pp. 327–328.

ACKNOWLEDGMENTS

Some poems in *TENDER* first appeared in the following publications.

1 "on heroics," *Mix* 22, no. 4 (Spring 1997).
2 "notes towards a body I (mozambique)," *The Capilano Review* 2, no. 24 (Winter 1998).
3 "*untitled I*" was commissioned as a postcard by the Burnaby Art Gallery in 2000, reproduced in *West Coast Line* in 2001, and reprinted as a postcard in 2004 for the Morris and Helen Belkin Art Gallery's exhibition *Re-Reading the 80s: Feminisms as Process in Vancouver*, curated by Jessie Caryl.
4 "LUNG: towards embodying," in *DAMP: Contemporary Vancouver Media Arts*, ed. Oliver Hockenhull and Alex Mackenzie (Vancouver, B.C.: Anvil Press, 2008).
5 "untitled II" is inspired by photographs by Sharyn Yuen and appeared in *Facing History: Portraits from Vancouver*, ed. Karen Love (Vancouver, B.C.: Presentation House Gallery and Arsenal Pulp Press, 2002). It is the third instalment in a series of writings first published in *West Coast Line* 32, 34, no. 3 (Spring 2001). The second instalment can be found in *Mix* 27, no. 2 (Fall 2001). My appreciation to Sharyn Yuen for her photographs. Written in memory of my grandmother Yuen Ip Hong (1911–2001).
6 "notes towards a body II," in *Swallowing Clouds: An Anthology of Chinese-Canadian Poetry*, ed. Andy Quan and Jim Wong-Chu (Vancouver, B.C.: Arsenal Pulp Press, 1999).
7 "to gut and a rise," *West Coast Line* 38, 36, no. 2 (Fall 2002).
8 "what is a park?," *Cube* 1 (December 1996).
9 "whale," *West Coast Line* 69 (Spring 2011).
10 *she who had scanned the flower of the world ...*, single artist's book, 1996, collection of the Morris and Helen Belkin Art Gallery.

THANKS

For my granny Yuen Ip Hong, my father Chu Yao Chung, and my sister Rose.

To my mother Chin Kow, for keeping us afloat all our lives, and now to roam her flower garden of abundance.

To my sisters Fay King and Fay Wah for introducing me to art and poetics in early childhood, with my other siblings and in building kinships, with a tender love and a freeing wildness.

Gratitude to Debora O, Cecily Nicholson, Charles Simard, Catriona Strang, andrea bennett, and all at Talonbooks.

To Daphne Marlatt and Colin Browne for their supportive encouragement, to Jan Clausen and Mariana Romo-Carmona for long-term friendships in writing and activisms, to Jamila Ismail and Ellie Epp for finding me those many years back – and meeting Jam in the downtown VCC cafeteria for the first time when she blew openings into my mind.

To Chrystos, for not vanishing, for in her she is, for courage and openings.

To Steve Bridger, trusty responder to my writing processes since we met as activists over thirty years ago.

For my friend Brice Canyon, a.k.a. McNeil (1960–2019).

To these unceded Lands, Territories, and Peoples of the xʷməθkʷəy̓əm, Sḵwx̱wú7mesh, and səl̓ilwətaʔɬ First Nations for providing me home and refuge since 1977.

Circa 1968, Rezende Street (Harare, Zimbabwe). Photographer unknown.

LAIWAN is a visual artist, writer, activist, thinker, speaker, and educator in Vancouver, British Columbia. It has been said that she is reticent and modest, shying away from the spectacular, and these traits may belie the cosmopolitan and eclectic sources of her thought, as what she produces is so often surprising, even in its exploration of the ephemeral.

Her biography usually mentions a background of displacement; yet Laiwan has chosen to be based in Vancouver for decades, focusing on the local, where she is well known as an artist and as founder of the OR Gallery.

Of Chinese ancestry, she grew up first in apartheid Rhodesia (now Zimbabwe), with early schooling by German nuns; then, when her family relocated to Canada, she had the life of a teenager in East Vancouver, attending Britannia Secondary School where she learned to work the printing press. To make sense of things, she stumbled into poetry.

Educated at the Emily Carr College of Art and Design, encountering the punk and art-folk-rock music scenes, she later gained an M.F.A. from Simon Fraser University. She teaches in the United States.

www.laiwanette.net

(Biographical note composed by Steve Bridger.)